Manuela Haas

Proximity and distance

Manuela Haas

Proximity and distance

Professional behavior in helping relationships in social work

ScienciaScripts

Imprint

Cover image: www.ingimage.com

This book is a translation from the original published under ISBN 978-3-639-76014-9.

Publisher:
Sciencia Scripts
is a trademark of
Dodo Books Indian Ocean Ltd. and OmniScriptum S.R.L publishing group

120 High Road, East Finchley, London, N2 9ED, United Kingdom
Str. Armeneasca 28/1, office 1, Chisinau MD-2012, Republic of Moldova, Europe
Printed at: see last page
ISBN: 978-620-8-32104-8

The table of contents:

Chapter 1

1. Introduction

In my professional career, I worked for five years as a *socio-educational supervisor* in a round-the-clock, co-educational, social and experiential residential community for girls and boys aged 13 and over. The target group consists of young people with behavioral problems in the emotional, social and/or performance areas. Due to the problems, it is not possible for them to remain in their family of origin, as this is no longer responsible. As a *supervisor*, I was responsible for two young people as a confidant and contact person. The care approach is action- and resource-oriented. The focus of the work is on the interplay of intensive individual support, integrative experiential education and meaningful leisure activities.

In my mostly all-encompassing work as a caregiver, I was confronted with the issue of finding the right balance of closeness and distance to my profession and to my clients from the very beginning.

1.1 Research interest and research question

My interest in this topic developed in the course of my work in a shared flat. Especially in my role as a caregiver, I was able to learn how to establish helping contact with young people.

I worked very closely with the young people thanks to the care system. In order to create the right and important distance, I needed to set myself apart, which was not always easy, especially at the beginning of my work. I tried to gain a position of trust, but still maintain my professionalism. As a result of reflecting on my own 3

Based on my own experiences and the behavior of other social workers, I decided to take a closer look at the tension between closeness and distance in helping relationships.

My aim in this paper is to show that "closeness and distance (...) is an unavoidable task, especially in social and educational fields of professional action" (Dörr/Müller 2007, p. 8). Professionals should be sufficiently capable of "(...) artfully interweaving and mediating closeness and distance to their addressees and their problems" (ibid., p. 8). In order to counteract "burn-out" and "blunting" within the professional activity, the question arises *as to how helpers can cope with the closeness-distance problem and avoid an imbalance of this polarity in helping relationships in social work.* In my literature research, I came across *reflective competence* and *authenticity*, topics that professionals inevitably have to deal with in order to act professionally in this area of tension.

1.2 Structure of the work

The following work comprises three chapters. While the first two chapters represent an approach to the topic, the third chapter relates explicitly to my research question.

In the **first chapter**, I deal with the question *"What is professional?"* and with the professional attitude that transports professional action and brings it to light. I then go on to discuss two professional models that illustrate the consequences of different theoretical approaches. Both models are "(...) significant for the discourse on professional theory in social work (...)" and have "(...) led to divergent assessments of the degree of professionalization and the fundamental professionalizability of this profession (...)" (Heiner 2004, p. 17). At the end of the first chapter, I outline a selected framework model of successful professional action.

In order to move on to the aspects of a professional relationship, I start the **second chapter** by looking at what a relationship is, i.e. a general definition of a relationship, and differentiate between role relationships and personal relationships from everyday psychology. I then draw on Carl R. Rogers' experiences with his clients in order to better understand the basic elements of a successful helping relationship. From these experiences, he developed conditions that are essential for a functioning helping relationship. I will take a closer look at the four elements of a helping relationship that are important to him, namely congruence, empathy, appreciation or positive affection and unconditional acceptance. I then examine the concept of transference and countertransference with regard to its significance for social work, which is a particular difficulty that the helper is repeatedly exposed to in the relationship with their clients. At the end of the third chapter, I deal with relationship work and the working alliance in order to show that relationship work is an everyday, practical necessity in professional helping relationships. In this context, I will also talk about the working alliance, which represents agreements between specific people and clarifies the framework conditions within which a relationship can develop (cf. Bimschas/Schröder 2003, p. 22). Every human relationship has to deal with polarities that need to be kept in balance. This is how

The third chapter addresses the polarity of closeness and distance. At the beginning of this chapter, I try to conceptualize the concepts of closeness and distance in pedagogical fields of work. According to Dörr and Müller (2007, p. 8), closeness and distance "(...) are considered an unavoidable task, especially in social and pedagogical fields of professional action. In contrast to everyday actions, professionals should be able to "(...) artfully interweave and mediate closeness and distance to their addressees and their problems" (ibid., p. 8). In the next step, I will deal with the topic of the balance between closeness and distance and the fact that this pair of terms requires each other in order to be used meaningfully (cf. Stierlin 1972, p. 62). In the following, I will address the issue of an imbalance between closeness and distance and, in doing so, "professional burnout" in social work. An inadequate balance of closeness and distance can lead to "burnout" on the part of the helper, to a "blunting" of their actions within the professional activity and even to leaving the profession. At the end of the fourth chapter, I will highlight opportunities for professionals that can promote successful handling of the proximity-distance problem. In addition to many other competencies, I have chosen to explain reflective competence and authenticity in more detail in my literature research.

At the end, there is a summary in which the results and findings resulting from the work are summarized and an outlook.

In my paper, the terms social worker and social pedagogue are used in parallel. I would also like to point out that in some of the literature only the masculine form was used, which can be seen in the literal quotations.

Chapter 2

2. Professional action in social work

"Social work has problems proving its services and quality to the public and also to itself, although it has become widely established in the last 20 years and has become an integral and natural part of modern municipal infrastructure in the course of its increasing normalization" (Heiner 2004, p. 7).

This makes it all the more important for me personally to respond to these deficits and to make it clear that professional action can be realized in good practice. In the following, I will deal with the question *"What is professional?"* and with the *professional attitude* that transports *professional action* and brings it to light.

2.1 Professional action - An approach to the terminology

l/Vas *is professional?* - Herwig-Lempp (2003, p. 10) believes that theories and an orientation towards the requirements of social work practice are needed to provide an answer to this question. The term expresses this,

- "(...) that this is an activity that requires certain **knowledge and skills** [emphasis in original] required (...)
- that this is recognition for the **quality** [emphasis in original] of the work performed or that a certain quality standard can be expected
- that someone **earns a living** through the activity [emphasis added bung in the original] (ibid., p. 10).

Herwig-Lempp (2003, p. 10) states that a small concept for what is considered professional has thus been developed. As further or more precise characteristics of professionalism, he lists

- the training
- the methods and tools of the profession
- the professional reflection
- the organization
- the money
- customer orientation
- the order clarification
- the quality of the work
- the limits of responsibility

(cf. Herwig-Lempp 1997, quoted from: Herwig-Lempp 2003, p. 10).

In order to get closer to the concept of professional action, I will now look at the *professional attitude* in social work, which transports and brings to light the socio-pedagogical action.

Profession comes from the Latin (*professio*) and means confession, trade, business, public declaration (cf. Mührel 2008, p. 62). *"Professio*, in turn, comes from the Latin *profiteri*, which means nothing other than *to publicly declare oneself a profession"* (ibid., p. 62). Professionalization describes the process of "(...) *making oneself a profession* or *declaring oneself a profession"* (ibid., p. 62). Acting professionally means that someone approaches things in a professional manner (cf. ibid., p. 62). In terms of conceptual history, profession therefore does not initially refer to professionalism, quality or efficiency, but rather to a declaration, a commitment. A declaration or a commitment is preceded by the call of another. The answer lies in the declaration or commitment. There, an attitude is taken to this call. The profession is the expression and basis of this attitude. (cf. ibid., p. 63) Mührel (2008, p. 67) states that in this approach, profession presupposes and expresses an attitude. Without the call of another, there would be no reason for an attitude. The attitude that results from the call also awakens self-awareness and self-reflection with regard to the other. (cf. ibid., p. 67)

Speaking of a professional attitude often gives the impression that this attitude can be clearly distinguished from other attitudes. For example, the question arises as to what is meant by a non-professional attitude. (cf. ibid., p. 45) "To carry out the profession of social worker/educator, it is sufficient to have a good heart and common sense and to adopt a natural attitude towards the client" (ibid., p. 45). We often encounter such a naïve understanding from outsiders, but also from social work professionals, which is reason enough to get to the bottom of the question of a professional attitude (cf. ibid., p. 45).

Mührel (2008, p. 175) is of the opinion that attitude cannot be based solely on a kind of training of behavioral patterns. "(...) the thoughtful reflection of actions and the critical examination of theoretical knowledge" are also required (ibid., p. 175). According to Mührel (2008, p. 175), the professional attitude in social work is based on three pillars:

1. "Practical decision-making knowledge or intervention knowledge that the appropriateness of the intervention in relation to the situation and client.
2. Reflective knowledge as the intersection of intellectual insight into the own actions.
3. Scientific explanatory knowledge that helps people to reflect on their own action and its rationale and justification." (ibid., p. 175)

Specialist knowledge as well as methodological and diagnostic skills are essential for interventions that are appropriate to the situation and client (cf. ibid., p. 179). Mührel (2008, p. 179) states that there is a qualitative and quantitative difference between full-time and voluntary social work staff in terms of specialist knowledge. In order to develop and maintain a professional attitude, in addition to the general educational component, integration into social work discourses is of immense importance (cf. ibid., p. 179). This results in two requirements:

- "On the one hand, the willingness of the social pedagogue to regularly Participation in professional training and further education and
- on the other hand (...) the cultivation of general education" (ibid., p. 182).

Institutions must create a framework for further education and training that promotes and demands this. In order to maintain general education, professional helpers must have media skills, among other things.

Supervision also serves as an instrument for maintaining a professional attitude, which enables a review of socio-educational activities and a distancing from them. (cf. ibid., p. 182) "Supervision serves to

- the perfection of the instrumental skills of social pedagogues. dagogue with regard to their situation-appropriate application,

- the reflection of personal dispositions with regard to the socio-educational and their supportive integration into the same, and
- the reflection of role relationships in socio-educational work This brings the position within the occupational field structure into view" (ibid., p. 182).

For von Spiegel (2005, p. 594), the following rules can be recommended for a methodical approach that is oriented towards the scientific procedure:

- "Disclosure of the experience-based assumptions that underlie the situa and problem interpretations and actions;
- Reviewing your own experiences and convictions, for example by confronting different points of view or procedures, avoiding generalizations without considering the context;
- Forming and testing hypotheses on causes and effects;
- Adoption of scientific process skills - for example the Operationalization of goals or the systematic observation of one's own actions;
- Development of an 'experimental' attitude towards one's own Interventions - such as trying out and evaluating different approaches in relation to a goal;
- Documentation of the action steps as the basis for a revision on, professional public verifiability (transparency) and evaluation;
- Reference to theories
  - to expand or alternatively describe situations and problems (state knowledge);
  - to analyze and explain the typical nature of individual situations or problems (explanatory knowledge);
  - to justify goals (value knowledge);
  - in the construction and justification of causal relationships, including the anticipation and probable consequences of an intended action (procedural knowledge) (ibid., p. 594).

Müller and Becker-Lenz (2008, p. 28) write that professional action is often located in areas of tension and contradiction. This includes the transfer between theory and practice, the simultaneous existence of help and control in the intervention and the proximity-distance problem in the social relationship (cf. ibid., p. 28).

The consequences of different theoretical approaches are illustrated on the basis of two professional models described below. Both models are "(...) significant for the discourse on professional theory in social work (...)" and have "(...) led to divergent assessments of the degree of professionalization and the fundamental professionalizability of this profession (...)" (Heiner 2004, p. 17).

2.2 Structural profession model according to Oevermann

"The *structure-related profession model* by Oevermann (1996), based on Parsons, assumes three central components of professionalized activity:

(1) the expert knowledge,
(2) orientation towards the common good and
(3) the autonomy of the profession" (Oevermann 1978, 1996, p. 70ff, quoted from: Heiner 2004, p. 17)

These three factors are only present simultaneously in the classical professions and only they therefore achieve a professionalized reputation (cf. ibid., p. 17).

The prevailing assumption is that members of a profession practice their profession out of inner conviction and that the profession represents a "calling" for them and that practicing the profession gives meaning to their lives. For this reason, there is no talk of payment for their work, but rather of remuneration as a "fee" for their actions. By paying a fee, the client acknowledges the special service provided by the professional. The fee paid turns clients into contractual partners. They are therefore not just dependent recipients of a benefit. Dependence on payment reduces the unevenness of the relationship with the professional. Otherwise, they show only a limited willingness to negotiate their approach. Instead, she/he decides on the basis of her/his professional convictions. It should be noted that this asymmetry can only be reduced if clients are free to make their own decisions, i.e. if they can consult another therapist, doctor, lawyer and so on without disadvantages. (cf. Oevermann 1996, quoted from: Heiner 2004, p. 17f)

According to Oevermann (1996, cited in: Heiner 2004, p. 18), the role of the professional is characterized by the difficulty "(...) that it can neither be as diffuse, i.e. as all-encompassing, as a private relationship involving the whole person and all facets of their existence, nor as specific, i.e. related only to the solution of certain problems, as a public relationship.

functional, professional relationships are otherwise." Professionals are required to walk a tightrope between an all-encompassing and specific relationship (cf. ibid., p. 18).

In addition to the importance of training, for Oevermann (1996, cited in: Heiner 2004, p. 18) the development of a professional *"habitus"* is of immense importance for the self-control of members of the profession. "The habitus is a hybrid of professional ethos and professional routine. It should guarantee that professionals do not exploit the dependency of clients and always give their best." (ibid., p. 18) The professional habitus of professionals is based on core values that guide their actions, such as the autonomy and integrity of clients, a legal system based on a concept of justice and so on (cf. Müller/Becker-Lenz 2008, p. 36) Müller and Becker-Lenz (2008, p. 36) are of the opinion that an internalized professional ethos, i.e. a basic attitude specific to the profession, is indispensable for the practice of a profession. Professional ethics can be understood as the expression of a shared, profession-specific attitude. It forms the basis of the professional habitus and serves to guide the actions of professionals. (cf. ibid., p. 36) Müller and Becker-Lenz (2008, p. 35) consider the following components to be fundamental for a professional habitus in social work:

- "(...) a specific professional ethos,

- the ability to form a working alliance and
- the ability to understand cases with the inclusion of scientific of knowledge" (ibid., p. 35).

According to Oevermann (1996, cited in: Heiner 2004, p. 18), the way in which professionals solve problems consists in the combination of the general application of rules based on scientific knowledge and the empathic exploration of the particularities of the individual case, the "hermeneutic case understanding". According to Müller and Becker-Lenz (2008, p. 36), professionals must "(...) know the difference between explaining (using theoretical models) and understanding (the specific case) and be able to do both." Each case must be understood in its concreteness and uniqueness. It is important to consider each case in a differentiated way and not to subordinate it prematurely to a standardized theoretical structure. Case understanding must incorporate scientific findings and theories. The approach of professionals is based on reconstruction logic (reconstruction of the particularity of the specific case) and subsumption logic (use of theoretical models and abstract theories). (cf. ibid., p. 38) Oevermann (1996, quoted from: Heiner 2004, p. 18) describes this particular achievement as the *"representative interpretation"*. It represents the offer of a view of the problems which the client is not in a position to recognize, but which proves to be correct for him/her. The proxy interpretation cannot be standardized. Professional action can only be subjected to routines and controlled by administrative guidelines to a limited extent. (cf. ibid., p. 18f) For Oevermann (1996, quoted from: Heiner 2004, p. 19), the reason for the autonomy of professional action lies in this above-mentioned non-standardizability of the representative interpretation. Case understanding is seen as an intuitive skill, "(...) which is more than a learnable, retrievable 'manual' skill" (ibid., p. 19) This view corresponds to the self-conception of many social pedagogues that their professional actions are purely intuitive and not a "(...) justifiable, communicable

and controllable methodological approach (...)" (ibid., p. 19). Oevermann (1996, quoted from: Heiner 2004, p. 19) "(...) denies social work the status of a profession and thus also the right to act creatively at its own discretion.
Even if social workers find creative solutions on their own, these are "heroic special achievements" by individuals, as the this presupposes autonomy, which, according to Oevermann (1996, quoted from: Heiner 2004, p. 19), social work only achieves when social workers become independent. "According to Oevermann (Sahle 1985, p. 152, quoted from: Heiner 2004, p. 19), creative services and autonomous decisions are not compatible with the dependence of social work on the (state) administration, because such special services, ... are not covered by any institutionalized structure (...)." According to Oevermann (1996, quoted from: Heiner 2004, p. 19), social work can at best be a semi-profession, as its autonomy is often tied to the specifications and instructions of others, such as medical professionals, lawyers, administrative specialists and so on, as it has no clearly defined field of activity and no correspondingly defined, independent, scientific domain of competence.
Heiner (2004, p. 20) writes that "despite a now more action-theoretical and competence-related understanding of professionalization (.) aspects of Oevermann's model are still handed down in social work today and 'professionalism' (as a mode of action) (...) is closely linked to 'profession' (as a professional status)".

2.3 Action-oriented and competence-related professional model according to Schütze

The profession model according to Schütze"(.) concentrates more on the analysis of interaction processes as well as the intentions and strategies of those involved and their implementation" (Heiner 2004, p. 20). It is not the status of the profession in society, expressed for example through pay or public prestige, that is decisive, but the professional actions and problem-solving skills of the members of the profession. In contrast to the structural profession model, this model does not primarily refer to the characteristics of the old professions. Rather, it attempts to capture the characteristics of new professions empirically. (cf. ibid., p. 20) In contrast to Oevermann, for Schütze "(...) it is not clear from the outset that the simultaneous existence of the demands of the profession and the demands of the organization (including the state administration) must lead to the external determination of the professionals" (Heiner 2004, p. 20f). Rather, Schütze (1984, p. 319, quoted from: Heiner 2004, p. 21) is of the opinion that assistance "(...) in the form of organizational precautions is becoming increasingly necessary as the complexity of professional action problems grows", even if organizations tend to interfere in the problem solving of professionals and thus endanger their autonomy. Routines in organizations are viewed in a similarly ambivalent way. On the one hand, they prevent specific responses to clients; on the other hand, they provide security in the work process and contribute to standard results. (cf. Heiner 2004, p. 21) In contrast to Oevermann, Schütze (1984, pp. 354, 361f, quoted from: Heiner 2004, p. 21) sees social work as a profession "(...) that carries out an important social mission and (equipped with a bundle of 'powerful procedures') can and does intervene decisively in the lives of clients." Schütze (1984, p. 311f, 329, quoted from: Heiner 2004, p. 21) sees difficulties and paradoxes as characteristics of all professions.

In the current discourse on professional theory, professionalism is increasingly being differentiated from profession. While the profession model according to Oevermann only ascribes professionalism to those professions that exhibit all the characteristics of a profession, in the profession model according to Schütze, professional action, i.e. the actual performance of work, is decisive. (cf. Heiner 2004, p. 24) "In this respect, members of the 'semi-profession' of social work (...) can also act 'professionally' if they carry out the tasks of the profession - within the framework of socio-political guidelines - effectively and in accordance with professional standards" (ibid., p. 24).

In the following, I will go into more detail about this understanding of the profession and present a selected *framework model* of successful professional action by Heiner (2004).

2.4 A framework model for successful professional action

This model of professional action was created on the basis of the interpretation of 20 interviews with social work professionals and characterizes the basic criteria of professional action in social work (cf. Heiner 2004, p. 155). It represents an empirically developed framework model for analyzing and planning professional action in social work (cf. ibid., p. 161). "According to this model, every social work professional has to cope with six sets of requirements, albeit with different clients and at different times with different emphases" (ibid., p. 162):

1 .) Reflected partiality and helpful control as mediation between the individual and society

This first set of requirements is based on the intermediary function of social work. Conflicts between the individual and society arise when clients do not meet social expectations, but these still have to be fulfilled. Here, social work must position itself and mediate between the demands of society and the expectations of clients. This requires social work professionals to do more than just take the client's side with absolute empathy. The mediation of conflicting interests will only be successful if social and individual boundaries are taken into account. This includes the ability to guarantee the client the right degree of self-determination through support, while at the same time exercising sufficient control and possibly allowing the client to be controlled by others. It is also necessary to consider whether inclusion in social systems, such as family, school, work and so on, is necessary and helpful, or whether exclusion from such systems can no longer be avoided. The opposites between help and control should be balanced through the experience of helpful control. (cf. ibid., p. 162f)

2 .) Development of achievable and challenging goals in the face of uncertain prospects of success in under-structured fields of activity

Social work is often active in fields of activity with diffuse, unclear and undefined mandates and is therefore often unable to refer to a single, concrete and binding mandate. Social work professionals must largely determine their field of activity themselves. They set priorities, select forms of intervention, weigh up needs, enter into cooperation or not, tolerate violations of the norm or not, and so on. However, this wide scope of action does not apply to all fields of activity or individual tasks within a field of activity. For example, in the case of life-threatening neglect of an infant, the scope for action dwindles to almost zero if the infant has to be taken into care. (cf. ibid., p. 163) Heiner (2004, p. 163) states that "(...) most activities in most fields of work (...) are characterized by the under-structured nature of the field of activity and the diffuseness of the task".

In social work, achievable results cannot be clearly defined in advance in individual cases. This diffuse starting point and task situation makes it difficult to define goals. The danger lies in overtaxing oneself and the client, in measuring oneself against unrealizable goals or in being satisfied with a minimum of what is achievable instead of exploiting the full potential of each individual case. (cf. ibid., p. 163) According to Heiner (2004, p. 163f), overcoming these difficulties requires professionals to be able to "(...) position themselves appropriately between the poles of openness or structuring, excessive demands and insufficient demands (...)." In addition, participatory processes of goal setting should be initiated. Goal clarification and goal formulation must be negotiated with each client with a compromise between performance and consideration. (cf. ibid., p. 164)

3 .) Multi-professional cooperation and mediation of services for unclear and/or controversial professional profiles

This requirement is about asserting one's professional competencies, i.e. standards and convictions, in a multi-professional team or cooperating with other institutions in order to achieve a successful referral of clients. Both require the acceptance and respect of the professional standards and convictions of other institutions, but at the same time the professional should present a clear profile of their work and insist on the standards of their own profession in their actions. In order not to jeopardize the common orientation towards the cause, this should happen without constant confrontation or demarcation from other professional groups. An open, constructive and solution-oriented discussion as well as a possible division of tasks in dealing with a wide range of client problems are professional. (cf. ibid., p. 165)

5 .) Further development of the institutional and infrastructural framework conditions of a profession that is subordinate to the welfare state

This requirement includes the fact that social work can often only become active when other systems are overwhelmed or have already failed. An example of this would be the school, which can no longer cope with a disruptive child. As social work is a profession with a subordinate function in the welfare state, it is often called in late by other systems and can therefore only take very limited preventative action. For professional social workers, in addition to direct client work, productive exchange with various institutions and their representatives in the sense of lobbying for clients is of immense importance in order to enable and promote the further development of institutional and infrastructural framework conditions. Here, the professional stands between social interests or between the interests of other systems and his/her own professional interests. They must also show a willingness to critically analyze their own institution and advocate for improvements. (cf. ibid., p. 166)

6 .) Use of holistic and multi-perspective patterns of interpretation as a foundation for developmentally open problem-solving approaches on an empirical basis

This set of requirements relates to the ability to reflect. In order to repeatedly begin development processes with an uncertain outcome and to be able to deal with relapses, it is necessary to constantly examine one's own actions and actions on the basis of evaluation and scientific findings. The use of multidimensional and multi-perspective patterns of interpretation enables a holistic, deficit and resource-oriented approach. This helps to avoid a one-sided perspective. The object of reflection here is the client, the support system and one's own professional actions. In this context, reflection does not only mean improving one's own mental hygiene. (cf. ibid., p. 166f)

6 .) Task-oriented, participative relationship design and limited help in everyday situations

Social work is more confronted with the everyday lives of clients than neighboring professions. In contrast to everyday contacts and assistance, the timeframe and intensity are limited. The aim of this professional help is to enable clients to help themselves, to support and promote an increase in autonomy and ultimately to reduce or end the helpful relationship. The professional relationship requires a positioning between person-oriented and goal-oriented action and thus, among other things, a balance between closeness and distance. (cf. ibid., p. 164) "The asymmetry of the professional relationship requires special attention and sensitivity in order to find the right position between 'closeness and distance'" (Heiner, 2007, p. 470). During professional life, closeness to clients decreases, while distance increases. Over time, professionals develop the ability to spontaneously vary closeness and distance according to the situation (cf. ibid., p. 470). Heiner (2007, p. 470f) writes that newcomers to the profession often over-identify with their clients, whereas experienced professionals are often dominated by routine, resignation and sometimes even cynicism. Both cases lead to "burning out", i.e. burnout due to emotional exhaustion (see Chapter 4.3) (cf. ibid., p. 471). The right mix of symmetry and asymmetry is required in order to relieve, support and challenge clients and encourage them to take responsibility. The fundamentally asymmetrical relationship should be made symmetrical in certain phases and areas through participation and negotiation, so that a balance of flexibility and consistency is achieved. (cf. Heiner 2004, p. 164f)

In the following, I will refer to the last requirement mentioned by Heiner and examine the helping relationship in detail with regard to the aspect of closeness and distance. In doing so, I will work out what is meant by a *professional relationship*.

Chapter 3

3. The professional relationship

Creating helpful relationships is fascinating, lifelong work. All those who work in the field of human relations and try to understand this area are working on a problem that will determine the future. (Rogers 2000, p. 70f) Rogers (2000, p. 71) believes that the future will not depend on the natural sciences, but on us humans. In order to establish helpful relationships, we try to understand interactions, interpret them and deal with them (cf. ibid., p. 71). Only when I can establish a helpful relationship with myself can I enter into a helpful relationship with another (cf. ibid., p. 65).

In order to be able to move on to the aspects of a *professional relationship*, I will take a closer look at the term relationship below. *What is a relationship? What are the characteristics of a professional relationship? What significance does the relationship have in the helping process and which aspects are particularly important?*

3.1What is a relationship?

"Relationships are at the center of most plays, novels and films" (Asendorpf/Banse 2000, p. 1). For many people, relationships with other people are considered immensely important. At first glance, the field of relationships appears to be extremely confusing. The reason for this is the distinctions between the different types of relationships. (cf ibid., p. 1) "The fact that these relationship types nevertheless have many things in common that justify an overarching concept of relationship is a historically new finding in everyday psychology" (ibid., p. 1f). Asendorpf and Banse (2000, p. 2) state that to date there is no relationship psychology, but there is a wealth of research on the respective relationship types, such as partnerships, parent-child relationships, sibling relationships, relationships between children and their peers ("peer relationships"), friendships and relationships in professional life.

In the context of everyday psychology, a distinction is made between role relationships, i.e. functional relationships, and personal relationships. While the former result from reciprocal role expectations, the latter develop between two people because of their personality and not because of their social roles. (cf. ibid., p. 1) Both types of relationships consist of at least one dyad, i.e. two people, and have at least one stable pattern of interaction. Relationships usually have several interaction patterns. (cf. ibid., p. 4) The interaction pattern does not describe individual persons, but the dyad (cf. ibid., p. 3). Asendorpf and Banse (2000, p. 4) write that stable interaction patterns of a dyad indicate a relationship, "and conversely, relationships exhibit stable interaction patterns."

In the following, I will explain the above-mentioned distinction in everyday psychology *between role relationships and personal relationships* in more detail in order to be able to move on to the aspects of a professional relationship.

3.2Role relationships and personal relationships

"Role relationships are social relationships that are determined by the social roles of the two reference persons" (Asendorpf/Banse 2000, p. 7). Such relationships are defined by the roles performed and not by the people involved. When two strangers meet, it may take some time for a typical interaction pattern to form between them. (cf. ibid., p. 7) However, it can also be the case that a stable pattern of interaction emerges between two people from the outset, namely when both "(...) align their behavior with reciprocal *role expectations*" (ibid., p. 7). For example, negotiations between diplomats can remain the same from conversation to conversation, as the interaction partners only represent role bearers (cf. ibid., p. 7). "'Role' refers to a culturally determined expectation of interactional behavior" (ibid., p. 7). Such relationships are "impersonal". The individual roles can be assigned to different people without the interaction pattern being lost. The personality and history of the interaction have no effect on the relationship. (cf. ibid., p. 7) Nevertheless, Asendorpf and Banse (2000, p. 7) state that the longer role relationships last, the more likely it is that these relationships will become "more personal", i.e. that the attachment figures will begin to react to the personality of the other person and to the interaction history and its events. It is very difficult to prevent role relationships from developing into personal relationships (cf. ibid., p. 7).

"Personal relationships begin where explanations based on role behavior are no longer sufficient" (ibid., p. 8). If the social interaction between two people is not determined by roles, it is referred to as a personal relationship, such as a relationship between two friends who have no working relationship with each other (cf. ibid., p. 8). This form of relationship is "(...) exclusively a function of the continuous interaction between the personality of one person and the personality of the other *and* their shared history" (ibid., p. 8). Both contribute to a significant influence on their relationship. The interaction history of the caregivers is not only determined by the personality of those involved, but also by external events affecting the relationship. Such events can be influences from third parties, but can also be purely coincidental events that affect the further development of the relationship and help determine the course of a relationship. (cf. ibid., p. 8) Asendorpf and Banse (2000, p. 8) state that personal relationships "( ) are determined by the personality of both caregivers and external influences on the relationship (...)".

Most relationships are a mixture of role relationships and personal relationships (cf. ibid., p. 9).

3.1 The professional helping relationship

"(...) a relationship can be defined as helpful (...) when one of the participants endeavors to achieve for one or both parties that the latent inner resources of the individual are more highly valued, more sustainably expressed and more effectively used" (Rogers 2000, p. 53). Rogers (2000, p. 63) writes that helpful relationships have different characteristics than relationships that are not helpful. The attitude of the helping person and the perception of the person being helped are the main distinguishing features (cf. ibid., p. 63f). According to Rogers (2000, p. 63), an effective, helpful relationship is one in which the helper behaves congruently and transparently, is fully attentive to the client and understands the client's essential feelings as they appear to them.

In order to better understand the attitudinal or experiential elements that create a growth-promoting climate in a helping relationship, I will draw on Roger's (2007, p. 211ff) experiences with his clients. From these experiences, he developed conditions that are essential for a functioning and successful helping relationship.

3.3.1The interpersonal relationship as a fundamental element of conversation management according to Carl R. Rogers

Rogers (2007, p. 211) is convinced from his many years of practical work with people that in any profession where relationships between people are involved, "(...) the nature of the interpersonal relationship with the client is the most important element in determining success. Rogers (2007, p. 211f) states that regardless of whether the contact with the client is brief or long-term, the nature of the relationship is the element that releases and promotes development and growth.

In the following, I will go into more detail about the four elements of a helping relationship that are important to him, namely *congruence* (agreement with oneself), *empathy* (empathetic understanding), *appreciation or positive affection* and *unconditional acceptance.*

3.3.1.1Congruence (agreement with oneself)

According to Rogers (2007, p. 213), personal development is facilitated when the professional remains genuine and without a façade in the relationship with their clients. Rogers (2007, p. 213) describes this state as congruence with oneself, which means that the professional does not deny him/herself in the direct personal encounter and is completely him/herself.
According to Satir (1990, p. 131), in this type of reaction, all parts of a message go in the same direction, i.e. the words match the facial exprcssions, posture and vocal expression. This behavior makes relationships easy, free and honest and also hardly threatens the self-esteem of the person concerned. In people who behave congruently, messages are clear and direct, they reveal their feelings unhindered, are able to move freely, express the truth in the moment, say what they would like to do and thus show integration and openness.

You feel comfortable in the presence of such people and you trust them because you know from their behavior where you stand with them. (cf. ibid., p. 131ff) The congruent way of responding is a way of reacting to real people in real situations that makes it possible to agree or disagree with someone based on one's own feelings (cf. ibid., p. 137). Assumptions based on practical experience mean that congruent behavior is most likely to be found in only one percent of the population (cf. ibid., p. 139).

The more genuine the professional is in the client relationship and the stronger the agreement with him/herself, the more likely it is that the client's personality will change (cf. Rogers 2007, p. 213). Rogers (2007, p. 214) writes that helpers should prefer to remain genuine, even when dealing with negative feelings towards clients, rather than putting on a façade that does not correspond to reality. However, according to Rogers (2007, p. 214), this is not easy to achieve. For Rogers (2007, p. 215), the element of congruence represents "(...) a highly important, indeed possibly (...) the most decisive among the other conditions to be described (...)". Nevertheless, this element is neither easy to grasp nor to achieve (cf. ibid., p. 215).

3.3.1.2Empathy (empathic understanding)

For Rogers (2007, p. 216), empathy is "(...) feeling the client's inner world with its very personal meanings as if it were one's own (but without losing the quality of "as if") (...)". For him, empathy is the essence of a growth-promoting relationship. The professional develops a precise empathetic understanding of the client's personal world. If the helper succeeds in conveying an understanding of the client's personal world and is able to move freely within it, the professional can address the meanings in the client's experience of which they are usually unaware. Sensitive empathy can enable a person to come closer to themselves and learn to change and develop. When helpers absorb the client's world into their own, they run the risk of seeing life in the client's way and being changed themselves in the process, which leads to helpers analyzing and evaluating, but not understanding, as a protection against this. (cf. ibid., p. 216f) Rogers (2007, p. 217) is of the opinion that change occurs when the professional sees and feels like the client, "(...) without losing the autonomy of his/her identity in this process of empathy." Furthermore, Rogers (2007, p. 217) argues that the mere communication of the professional's willingness to empathize is enough, understanding their client(s) is very useful and can be appreciated. "None of us can maintain such empathy (...), but we can certainly develop in this direction" (ibid., p. 217).

3.1.1.1 Appreciation or positive attention

In order to promote further development, it is extremely important for Rogers (2007, p. 218) that the professional "(...) adopts a warm, positive and accepting attitude towards the client's processes." The professional cares for their clients in a non-possessive way and respects them as individuals in their own right (cf. ibid., p. 218). For Rogers (2007, p. 218), this represents a type of affection that has strength and makes no demands. He chooses the term "positive affection" for this (cf. ibid., p. 218).

3.1.1.2 Unconditional acceptance

Rogers (2007, p. 219) is of the opinion that the more unconditional the positive attention is, the more effective and successful a professionally helpful relationship will be. This means that the professional not only values their clients under certain conditions, but also gives them positive attention in a comprehensive manner. No judgment is made about the client. (cf. ibid., p. 219)

In summary, these were the aspects of a professional helping relationship as developed by Rogers.

The moment of *transference and countertransference* is a particular difficulty to which the helper is repeatedly exposed in the relationship with their clients. In the following, I will only deal with this concept in abbreviated form with regard to its significance for social work, as this would otherwise exceed the scope of my work.

3.4Transference and counter-transference

The terms transference and countertransference, which originate from psychoanalysis, can greatly overstress the relationship between closeness and distance in a relationship.

"In modern psychoanalysis, transference is generally understood as the repetition of acquired and internalized relationship patterns in the current interaction and situation. Countertransference refers to the emotional response, the specific reaction of the analyst to the transference of the analysand." (Stemmer-Lück 2004, p. 97) [In psychoanalysis, the professional is referred to as the analyst and the client as the analysand]. "What the analyst senses and experiences in the transference relationship is called countertransference" (ibid., p. 100). "Even if the analysand does not explicitly formulate how he perceives the analyst, the analyst has an idea, a feeling of how he is being experienced based on his countertransference" (ibid., p. 98). Transference and countertransference always belong together and form one aspect of the relationship dynamic. The analyst not only pays attention to the conflicts and issues inside and outside the setting, but also tries to grasp what is building up between him/her and the analysand. (cf. ibid., p. 97f) Different relationship feelings and role assignments are made transparent in this complex relationship structure (cf. ibid., p. 98).

According to Schmid (2007, p. 48), the concept of transference refers to two things in relation to the field of tension between closeness and distance: "The initial desire that arises for the analyst to grab them and kiss them creates a sudden and very vehement closeness. However, this closeness, with all its reactive shame and fear, initially leads to considerable disturbance and distance." Closeness and distance are dynamically linked in such experiences (cf. ibid., p. 48). Schmid (2007, p. 52) writes that transference is usually closely linked to a defensive process. Therefore, closeness refers to distance and vice versa (cf. ibid., p. 52f).

In social work, transference occurs in the relationship between client and social worker (cf. Stemmer-Lück 2004, p. 107). According to Stemmer-Lück (2004, p. 107), the concept of transference and countertransference is extremely useful, if not essential, in order to understand and act professionally. "In the direct relationship with the client, the social worker becomes involved in the specific transference/countertransference dynamic" (ibid., p. 108). This harbors the danger of acting unconsciously. Knowledge of the phenomenon of transference and countertransference is extremely necessary in order not to lose oneself in the interaction. This knowledge makes it possible to distance oneself, understand the dynamics and intervene appropriately. (cf. ibid., p.108) "The application of transference /Countertransference concepts are always particularly appropriate when the social worker reaches the limits of comprehensibility, when the client's behavior and experiences appear inappropriate, incomprehensible, irrational and when the social worker has become involved in conflictual, stressful relationships that limit his or her ability to reflect and act" (ibid., p. 108). Based on a precise analysis of the current situation by the helpers, they can gather a great deal of information, for example about
patterns from the past, as these are currently being repeated, albeit in a modified form. However, not only clients but also professionals repeat old patterns in the concept of transference and countertransference and help to shape the professional relationship. *What does the client trigger in me? What about me could have triggered the client's reaction?* It is always important to be able to answer both questions. This requires a high degree of self-awareness in professional social work. (cf. ibid., p. 110f)

Summarizing the concept of transference and countertransference, Schmid (2007, p. 57) states that it is a matter of "(...) getting the delicate entanglements of closeness and distance into thinking in practical work, of repeatedly transferring them into reflective thinking."

As mentioned at the beginning, consciously recognizing transference and countertransference is essential in professional *relationship work.* It is important that the moment of transference and countertransference in the *working relationship* is understood and controlled.

3.5Relationship work and working alliance

"'Relationship work' as a term often arouses the suspicion that it is supposed to be about a general feeling of well-being, about 'cuddly pedagogy' " (Bimschas/Schröder 2003, p. 10). Content and objectivity would only play a very subordinate role (cf. ibid., p. 10). There are also hardly any descriptions of the practice of everyday relationship work (cf. ibid., p. 17). For Bimschas and Schröder (2003, p. 15), relationship work does not represent an independent working approach. "(...) we see a meaningful approach to professional relationships in theory and practice when the relationships in the context of the activities and conditions and they are located as part of a working alliance (ibid., p. 15). Dörr (1996, p. 9) states that the term "relationship work" has become very popular in the psychosocial field in recent years. On the one hand, it is about "(...) the difficulty of separating the activity and the subjects working in this field from their work - it demands the whole person, not individual, functionally separable or temporally isolable skills and abilities - on the other hand (.)", "(.) the social value, the functionality of the educational activity for the social system as a whole" is emphasized (ibid., p. 9). Dörr (1996, p. 35) is of the opinion that relationship work represents a special form of service activity, whereby the social service referred to here is directly related to people. It is work with people, on people and directly for people. (cf. ibid., p. 35) For Bimschas and Schröder (2003, p. 9), relationship work represents "(.) an everyday, practical necessity in youth work". Methods, concepts and framework conditions can be developed, changed and tried out. Everyday relationship processes depend on the ability, intuition and unsuspiciousness of those involved and are therefore difficult to grasp theoretically. (cf. ibid., p. 9) For Bimschas and Schröder (2003, p. 10), whether and how people are reached is of central importance in pedagogical work. The goal of social work is to win the person over in order to be able to support and strengthen their development through contact and activities (cf. ibid., p. 20). "(.) Where interest and curiosity on the one hand are paired with experience, knowledge and a willingness to communicate on the other , learning takes place in social relationships" (ibid., p. 10). If the subject lacks any motivation, there is no learning process. The willingness to learn from someone and to engage with them over difficulties is very important. (cf. ibid., p. 19) If the professional leaves an impression on the client through their person, their behavior and their approach, they will have an effect on them (Gloel 2002, p. 45, quoted from: Bimschas/Schröder 2003, p. 18). However, a possible effect also depends on whether the clients accept and implement agreed goals and paths for themselves (von Spiegel 2002, p. 257, quoted from: Bimschas/Schröder 2003, p. 18f). Results cannot be predetermined in relationship work. The goal is not achieved by the measure, i.e. by the service offered, but by what it achieves or can achieve. (cf. Bimschas/Schröder 2003, p. 20) For Bimschas and Schröder (2003, p. 19f), rituals, the style of interaction and the transparency of rules are important prerequisites for the development of a sustainable relationship. Relationship work is about accepting boundaries and finding adequate and appropriate support. Conflict and confrontation are often unavoidable, which leads to a certain distance. (cf. ibid., p. 18). Professionals often have the impression that the usually very strenuous day-to-day relationship work is not adequately understood from the outside. If the relationship is brought to the forefront, professionals continue to struggle with skepticism and criticism. (cf. ibid., p. 16) Bimschas and Schröder (2003, p. 16) see the necessity of "(...) not separating work on *people and relationships* from work on *content and perspectives*." This is also the reason why many professionalization theorists regard the negotiation and maintenance of a working alliance as something very essential for the shaping of a pedagogical relationship (Finger-Trescher/Krebs 2001, p. 49, quoted from: Bimschas/Schröder 2003, p. 21). Müller (2000, p. 127, quoted from: Bimschas/Schröder 2003, p. 21) speaks of the fact that pedagogical relationships must be transformed into working alliances in order not to "lapse intolapse into therapeutization". Bimschas and Schröder (2003, p. 22) advocate that every development of new services should include the working relationship from the outset working alliance should be clearly formulated. "The working alliance represents the agreements between specific people and clarifies the framework conditions within which the relationship can develop" (ibid., p. 22). The working alliance makes the professional aspects of the relationship recognizable. In addition, the working alliance anchors the content side, i.e. professional measures and goals. (cf. ibid., p. 22) Müller and Becker-Lenz (2008, p. 37) report that working alliances prevent the danger "(...) that the help provided by social work professionals creates or maintains a dependency." Within a working alliance, clients must contribute to solving their problems themselves, depending on their degree of autonomy (cf. ibid., p. 37). According to Müller and Becker-Lenz (2008, p. 37), a working alliance is characterized by various features and rules that professionals must observe:

- "The voluntary nature or inner commitment to the working alliance, including under conditions of external coercion, must be guaranteed" (ibid., p. 37).
- Professionals and clients are whole persons and at the same time involved as role players. Clients' problems can only be solved if they are fully open to help and enter into a working alliance. In connection with the client role, they also have certain duties and tasks in the working alliance. Professionals are also involved as whole persons and must take an interest

in the client's crisis in order to understand its complexity. (cf. ibid., p. 37) "(...) what is not part of the role-specific fulfillment of the task" must be treated abstinently by professionals (ibid., p. 37).

- Helping people to help themselves is the principle of any working alliance. ses, which means that the clients have to cooperate and contribute (cf. ibid., p. 37f).
- Transference and countertransference must be understood in the working

alliance.

and controlled (cf. ibid., p. 38).

- Professionals have been protected by law and political will.
  They must adhere to their mandate, but in fulfilling their mandate they are completely committed to their clients (cf. ibid., p. 38).

Ultimately, the question arises *as to whether relationship work can be learned or whether it is a given?*

For Herwig-Lempp (2003, p. 12), relationship work can be learned. Social workers should have the ability to shape relationships with their clients in such a way that they support the process of help and counseling in the best possible way. (cf. ibid., p. 12) Herwig-Lempp (2003, p. 12) states that this ability is often seen as something given, but by no means as something acquired or appropriated. Relationship work "(...) is based on theoretical considerations and thus also the possibility of exerting methodological influence, even if this is often not consciously recognized. (Conversely, it very quickly becomes clear how a relationship can be negatively influenced...)" (ibid., p. 12). Client relationships can be actively shaped by social workers, which they are not always necessarily aware of (cf. ibid., p. 12). Relationships can be fostered through concrete action and an appropriate attitude, "(.) e.g. through

- the consideration and recognition of the different per

perspectives of those involved,

- the recognition and appreciation of their respective autonomy (voluntary where possible) and their stubbornness (personal view and interests),
- the consideration of exceptions to the problem,
- focus on resources, skills, strengths and successes,
- the question of wishes and expectations and by developing the fulfillment of orders,
- working on the formulation of goals and solutions of the clients,
- the skillful use of compliments and other methods of appreciation" (ibid., p. 12f).

Herwig-Lempp states that the ability to establish relationships can be captured theoretically and thus also made methodologically manageable (cf. ibid., p. 13). It is nothing "(...) of which one can say, 'one has it, the other doesn't' (...)" (ibid., p. 13).

Every human relationship has to deal with polarities that need to be kept in balance. In the following, I will talk about the *polarity of closeness and distance.*

Chapter 4

4. Proximity and distance - A polarity in helping relationships

Within a helping relationship, it is essential to work with the right balance of closeness and distance, which contributes significantly to the success of helping relationships. In the following, I will take a closer look at this specific aspect of a professional relationship. As a basis for this, I will return to Rogers and his conditions for a functioning and successful helping relationship. As he did not use the terms closeness and distance in his elements of a helping relationship, I will now try to introduce these into his hypotheses myself:

Congruence, i.e. the authenticity and lack of facade of the professional towards their client, is part of the aspect of closeness in a professional helping relationship. The word closeness describes familiarity, knowing and understanding each other in a relationship, but this is only successful if both parties are authentic and do not put on a façade.
Roger's empathic understanding, i.e. *empathy,* includes a further aspect of closeness. By taking in the client's world, the helper achieves an emotional closeness to the client. The distance comes to light here through the "as if" formulated by Rogers. The "as if" requires the helper to maintain professional distance and a view of the whole.

What do closeness and distance mean for helping relationships? What influence do professionals and clients have on this?
My work is about the tension between *closeness and distance* between helpers and clients, i.e. the polarity of closeness and distance in the helping relationship, which I will deal with below. First of all, I would like to add that it is difficult to find a

precise definition of the polarity of closeness and distance in the literature.

4.1Proximity and distance - An approach to the field of tension

The relationship between professional helpers and clients plays an important role in working with people. The resulting difficulty in achieving adequate closeness and distance is a general issue for those working in social work. This area of tension is a significant aspect of everyday social work and is an important basis for the work of all professionals. The mediation of closeness and distance is inevitably one of the tasks of professional action.

Dörr and Müller (2007, p. 8) write that professional action should differ from everyday action in that the professional has the ability to combine and mediate closeness and distance to their clients and their problem situations.

Nagel (2000, p. 366ff, quoted from: Dörr/Müller 2007, p. 9) is of the opinion that the professional is only in a position to understand the problem situations of his/her clients if he/she does not act in a role-based manner, "(....) but uses their intuitive and personal power of experience ('closeness') to provide a 'diffuse offer of understanding', which at the same time is supported by a distanced attitude of acceptance by the other party ('distance')."

Thiersch (2007, p. 29) is of the opinion that the question of closeness and distance is an everyday issue in social work. "Some insist on closeness, i.e. that socio-pedagogical action is determined by the quality of the relationship work, getting involved, building trust (.)" and "others see the professional ability to distance as the actual characteristic of socio-pedagogical action (.)" (ibid., p. 29). The different relationship patterns in everyday life are characterized by closeness and distance.

The success of closeness presupposes the existence of distance and, conversely, distance succeeds where it can relate to closeness. (cf. ibid., p. 31f) Thiersch (2007, p. 35) writes that recipients need both the experience of attachment and the imposition of self-activity, which means a special form of closeness and distance. People in the process of becoming are dependent on acceptance, acceptance and unconditional love. At the same time, they need the freedom to shape their own lives. This interaction, characterized by extreme closeness and distance, is precarious. Adolescents are dependent on the educator and at the same time endangered by him/her. (cf. ibid., p. 35) Thiersch (2007, p. 43) also states that closeness and distance in action is discussed as a question of boundaries in action. It is impossible to act without clarifying mutual expectations and possibilities. Agreements and contracts secure the freedom of the addressees in the power structure of pedagogical interventions. At the same time, the agreements and contracts must be secured against quick suggestions from professionals. Negotiating these between the professional and the client requires patience. (cf. ibid., p. 43)

Müller (2007, p. 141) is of the opinion that professional working relationships are both close and distant at the same time. In this train of thought, he cites the example of the analyst. He/she knows the client's most intimate secrets and areas of greatest vulnerability, but remains completely detached from their everyday lives and exerts no influence or power over them. (cf. ibid., p. 141) Both are in an extremely intimate relationship. They desire each other and fight with each other. This happens on an unconscious emotional level beyond the control of the mind. However, this is only possible and does not lead to emotional chaos because it takes place within a working alliance in which abstinence is the basic rule. The extraordinary closeness of the therapeutic process is excluded from "real life" and is embedded, for example, in the hourly act. The analyst is responsible for the boundary between intimacy in the therapeutic process and intimacy in real life. The client has the right to break the boundaries within this framework at any time. The client can, at his/her own responsibility, try out in real life the experiences he/she has had in the therapeutic process. The analyst must be able to tolerate not helping them to do so. (cf. ibid., p. 145)

Throughout their history, all professions have developed strategies to enable a distancing that at least symbolically neutralizes the dangers of too much closeness. Examples of this would be technical language, "white coats" and so on. (cf. ibid., p. 141f) Müller (2007, p. 142) writes that such distancing in the field of professional action can be extremely beneficial to people. Someone in distress usually attaches particular importance to the confidentiality, neutrality and objectivity of professional treatment and perhaps also to a symbolically oriented aura of professional helpers. (cf. ibid., p. 142)

Müller (2007, p. 149) also states that coping with everyday life is not only the task of the helpers, but also that of the organization. He cites, for example, the "induction period" for new employees, concepts for anticipated crisis situations and so on (cf. ibid., p. 149)

In the field of home education, according to Müller (2007, p. 155), "(...) the risk of unmanageable closeness is not only the greatest danger, but also, if the risk is accepted and overcome, the greatest source of opportunity." The same applies to accepting inner distance that is difficult to bear. Coping with closeness cannot be achieved organizationally or pedagogically. It arises from the ability to allow the unexpected. (cf. ibid., p. 155)

For Schmid (2007, p. 57), the aim is to show "(...) how, from a psychoanalytical perspective, closeness and distance are related to each other and linked in a complex and non-resolvable way." There is no escape from this in both educational and therapeutic contexts. It is important to incorporate the intricacies of closeness and distance into thinking and to constantly reassess them in a reflective way. (cf. ibid., p. 57)

Klatetzki (2007, p. 83) writes that the pole of distance is located in the reflective team meetings. Closeness is understood as "front-line" interaction. Reflection with colleagues therefore serves to (re-)establish a person's self. From this perspective, the interweaving and mediation of closeness and distance helps professionals to cope with the emotional stresses to which they are repeatedly exposed on the "front-line". (cf. ibid., p. 83) The effect of this scheme is not direct, but indirect: "By stabilizing and consolidating threatened identities, the use of the difference between closeness and distance also prepares a professional approach to clients" (ibid., p. 83).

Bimschas and Schröder (2003, p. 28) write that a large number of communication problems in a relationship result from what is perceived as close or distant. It is important to bring movement into the relationship, which means not clinging to a fixed idea of distance, but allowing more closeness in order to be able to work through any entanglements. Closeness is always associated with dangers that we cannot escape when we find ourselves in human relationships. An encounter or contact with the other is only possible if you bring in your own feelings, which means that you are no longer distanced. (cf. ibid., p. 28) "(...) if one does not have the tools to orient oneself in relationships with others and to distinguish what belongs to whom, then one swings back and forth between the two extreme poles, that of great closeness associated with the danger of fusion and that of great distance associated with the danger of becoming indifferent to the other" (ibid., p. 29).

In the following, I will discuss the *balance between closeness and distance* and show that this cannot be taken for granted in everyday life and is always precarious. Professional helpers must try to maintain an adequate distance from their clients. This should nevertheless allow for a constructive working relationship for both sides.

4.1 Balance of closeness and distance

The right balance of closeness and distance is extremely important in any relationship. Professional action can only be achieved with a balance of closeness and distance.

Bimschas and Schröder (2003, p. 24) assume "(...) that a person's ability to relate is determined by their 'separateness'". It is about "staying with oneself" within a relationship. The decisive factor is how separate we feel from the other person. If the boundary between two people is missing and the closeness is too great, our own identity becomes blurred. Where it is not clear whether we are dealing with our own wishes and needs or those of the other person, there is an overlap. The result is a restriction of the ability to act towards the other person. There is no secure standpoint from which a person can establish or enter into relationships. The result is a complete appropriation and a deferral of one's own needs. (cf. ibid., p. 24)

We find closeness in all our interpersonal relationships. However, this closeness always harbors dangers, such as disappointment, hurt, being betrayed or, as mentioned at the beginning, giving up oneself and one's own needs.

According to Stierlin (1972, p. 62), "the concepts of proximity and distance (...) presuppose each other in order to be used meaningfully. The closest proximity that is conceivably possible still presupposes a certain distance between two objects. If this residual distance is missing, then proximity becomes fusion and the term proximity is no longer applicable." (ibid., p. 63) Proximity and distance denote a distance, but do not represent an absolute quantity. What appears close to one person can be distant to another and vice versa.
Closeness and distance are real in every relationship (cf. ibid., p. 63). To illustrate this, Stierlin (1972, p. 63) draws on the three Hegelian moments of relationship:

-Desire-enjoyment

-Work and

-fear of death

These moments are essential for the significance of the polarity of closeness and distance.

Desire and pleasure in a relationship require closeness and distance. Desire and pleasure seek closeness, but also distance from one's own needs and from the other person who is able to satisfy these needs. Closeness can only be found again and again through the work of distancing. Through psychological and emotional distancing, we can recognize the other person in their otherness. From time to time, the emotional bond with the other person must be "broken" in order to understand them. This distancing work is difficult, as it brings up feelings of loneliness and being an outcast. (cf. ibid., p. 63) Stierlin (1972, p. 64) writes that distancing work is difficult and painful, that it can be compared to approach work and that both distancing work and approach work are always required of us. This over-

These considerations lead to the third Hegelian relational moment, namely the fear of death (cf. ibid., p. 64). The fear of death represents a borderline experience, "(...) which is the condition for essential steps of maturation" (ibid., p. 64). The danger of this experience and the possibilities of overcoming it seem to be particularly linked to the polarity of closeness and distance. In a relationship, each of the two partners must dare to awaken their archaic childhood fears in order to find a balance between dependence and independence. (cf. ibid., p. 64) "Closeness to the other conjures up (...) the danger that early childhood greed, insatiability and destructiveness will reawaken and be directed against the person to whom we have made ourselves helpless and thus in a certain sense restored our childhood dependence" (ibid., p. 64). Stierlin (1972, p. 64) writes that we have to take the risk of losing our ego boundaries, thereby exposing ourselves to an inner terror and,

through "(...) the fear of madness, opening the door to madness itself."

I would like to point out here that Stierlin does not speak of a professional relationship, but that interpersonal processes play a role in all relationships and are not only recorded with regard to professional relationships.

Bimschas and Schröder (2003, p. 24) write that too much affection appears like an assault in which the ego boundaries are violated. The boundary to the other is experienced as diffuse and permeable (cf. ibid., p. 24). According to Bauriedl (1994, p. 106, quoted from: Bimschas/Schröder 2003, p. 24), the greater the overlap between two people, the more serious the relationship disorder or mental illness in a relationship. A person who was exposed to constant abuse in childhood has difficulty distinguishing between self and other, which means that it is difficult for them to recognize their own wishes, feelings and fears and to distinguish these from those of others. The person finds it difficult to look at themselves and therefore tends to confuse themselves with other people. (cf. Bimschas/Schröder 2003, p. 24f)

Bimschas and Schröder (2003, p. 25) state that the experience and perception of separateness and difference is a particularly important prerequisite in a relationship. If I constantly enter into overlaps, I do not perceive the other person as the other person at all and therefore do not have a "real relationship" with the other person. The result of this would be a sharing of myself, which leads to confusion and misunderstandings. (cf. ibid., p. 25) "On a positive note, the aim in relationships should be to be able to recognize and maintain the personal boundaries of one's own person" (ibid., p. 25). This can lead to a perception of the differences between relationship partners and a differentiation between oneself and the other person. In order to develop a clear identity, the boundaries must be visible and tangible for the growing child. In addition, the interplay of closeness and distance must be tested and both poles must be recognized. (cf. ibid., p. 25)

Bimschas and Schröder (2003, p. 25) summarize that this ideal state outlined above does not always exist in relationships, but it does show what needs to be taken into account when shaping relationships with regard to closeness and distance and their balance.

Thiersch (2007, p. 32) writes that achieving a balance between closeness and distance in everyday life is not always a matter of course, but is often very difficult. Closeness leads to clinging relationships (cf. ibid., p. 32). "Distance, in turn, leads to the coexistence of indifference, overlooking and carelessness, and thus to placelessness in everyday life" (ibid., p. 32).

Finding a balance between closeness and distance is a major challenge for professionals, which they are confronted with more or less on a daily basis in their practice.

In the following, I will deal with *burnout syndrome in social work*, which is a work-related mental illness that can develop when there is an insufficient balance between closeness, i.e. commitment and distance, and which shows the relevance of the right balance.

4.2 Imbalance of closeness and distance

A lack of boundaries towards clients and the profession leads to overstressing of professionals, which is expressed in mental illness, inadequate behavior and possibly also in flight from work.

Professional work with people is difficult, stressful and rarely rewarded. Professional helpers are constantly confronted with situations that require both care and empathy, i.e. distance and closeness. Committed people in particular are not immune to the phenomenon of burning out. (see Reiners-Kröncke/Röhrig/Specht 2010, p. 7f)

In order to make the importance of the balance between closeness and distance in helping professions transparent, I will now outline this occupational disease as an example.

Burnout literally means to burn out. In the context of helpers, this term was coined by Freudenberger (1974) in the USA. (cf. Schmidbauer 2007, p. 322) Burning out means "emptying oneself". Exhausting one's own physical and mental reserves. (cf. Reiners-Kröncke/Röhrig/Specht 2010, p. 10) According to Farber (1983, quoted from: Reiners-Kröncke/Röhrig/Specht 2010, p. 29f), burnout is "(...) a state of fatigue or frustration caused when the person concerned becomes involved in a case, a way of life or a relationship that does not bring the expected reward." Burnout occurs in the context of working with other people (see Reiners-Kröncke/Röhrig/Specht 2010, p. 34). Empathy, emotional confrontation and intensive commitment can cause enormous emotional stress for professional helpers (cf. ibid., p. 36). Freudenberger initially used the term burnout to describe committed social workers, psychologists and doctors in independent clinics, "(...) who often showed symptoms of exhaustion and fatigue after a short time" (Reiners-Kröncke/Röhrig/Specht 2010, p. 10). Sources of burnout are over-motivation and illusionary expectations (cf. Schmidbauer 2007, p. 323). The core of burnout is "(...) the stress caused by work-related contact with other people (...)" (Gusy 1995, quoted from: Reiners-Kröncke/Röhrig/Specht 2010, p. 12). The emotionally demanding and exhausting interaction with people can be seen as a causative factor. Factors for this include role conflicts and role ambiguity. (see Reiners-Kröncke/Röhrig/Specht 2010, p. 28) Burnout is a gradual and protracted process. There is still no consensus among experts on the duration of the process. (cf. Reiners-Kröncke/Röhrig/Specht 2010, p. 14) According to Gusy (1995, Reiners-Kröncke/Röhrig/Specht 2010, p. 14), burnout processes can occur several times in a lifetime.

Schmidbauer (2007, p. 324) writes that in the *initial phase*, overcommitment, i.e. a lack of distance, is one of the first signs of burnout. In order to fulfill the helping role, those affected are overactive, they feel indispensable and their own needs are

denied (cf. ibid., p. 324). This leads to confusion between commitment and dedication (cf. Reiners-Kröncke/Röhrig/Specht 2010, p. 32). "(...) the helpers compensate for their personal problems and needs with increased professional commitment" (ibid., p. 32). However, this compensation cannot be maintained over a longer period of time. For example
confusing their own needs with those of the client can lead to over-identification. Defining boundaries is difficult, but absolutely necessary. If the helper does not differentiate between adequate commitment and over-commitment, this leads to a dissolution of the boundary between the client's life and that of the helper. (cf. ibid., p. 32)

In the *slump phase*, this façade of performance eventually collapses. Aspirations and experiences of success diverge. Those affected are confused and uncertainty about their role spreads. Increasing distance from their own tasks and from the people in their care are symptoms of this. Cynicism in dealing with clients prevails. (cf. ibid., p. 324f) Negative changes occur in direct contact with clients, such as a loss of positive feelings towards clients (cf. Reiners-Kröncke/Röhrig/Specht 2010, p. 14). Other warning signs are chronic tiredness, reluctance to take up work, little private life, restricted contacts, restricted interests and unsatisfactory leisure activities. The work is perceived as more strenuous, more responsible and also worse paid than all other activities. Those affected feel exploited.

This phase of exhaustion and disadvantage can be followed by a reduction in performance in the *decline phase*. The willingness to perform and commitment diminish. As those affected no longer have any distance to their work and their clients, they become unable to criticize. In addition to depressive symptoms, physical ailments also occur. Alcoholism and drug abuse are not uncommon. In their private lives, those affected withdraw from contact and become lonely. (cf. Schmidbauer 2007, p. 325ff) Schmidbauer (2007, p. 328) writes that the *final phase* of burnout development is a rare extreme case. Rather, those affected conceal their inner withdrawal from the job by working according to the rules (cf. ibid., p. 328).

It should be noted that to date there are only preliminary assumptions about the causes, symptoms and course of burnout (see Reiners-Kröncke/Röhrig/Specht 2010, p. 18).

For Schmidbauer (2007, p. 329), the most important protection against burnout is constant professional development. "Those who can develop professionally do not burn out" (ibid., p. 324). Team development and supervision repeatedly provide confirmation of this. For Reiners-Kröncke, Röhrig and Specht (2010, p. 39), it is of utmost importance in prevention that helpers set internal and external boundaries between work and their private lives in order to prevent the occurrence of burn-out syndrome.

Having outlined the problem of the professional helper's boundaries to their clients, it is extremely important to me in my work to highlight opportunities for professionals that can promote a successful approach to the proximity-distance problem. In addition to many other competencies, I have decided in my literature research to explain *reflective competence* and *authenticity* in more detail below.

4.3 Opportunities for professional management of the proximity-distance problem

For me personally, reflective competence and authenticity are skills that ensure that closeness does not lead to clinging intimacy and distance does not lead to indifference and escape. In order to be able to create a balance between closeness and distance to clients and to act professionally in this area of tension, it is of immense importance that helpers consciously deal with reflexive competence and authenticity, among other things.

4.3.1 Reflective competence

"Reflective competence means the ability of the social pedagogue not to lose or deny their own development in its formative traces, but to integrate it into their professional actions" (Geißler/Hege 2001, p. 229). The term "self-awareness" describes this in its original meaning (cf. ibid., p. 229). "Self-conscious in this sense is someone who, as someone who has become, does not allow their own development to be submerged" (ibid., p. 229). One's own personality traits are expressed and become effective within the professional activity. The interaction of helpers with their clients is determined by previous experiences that influence their professional actions. (cf. ibid., p. 229) Their professional identity can "(...) only ever be experienced as successful on the basis of previous experiences, their reflection and critical reappraisal (...)" (ibid., p. 229). This represents subjectivity in professional action. Current sensitivities of helpers in situations can often only be explained and understood by looking back at past life experiences. If the analysis and processing of one's own life story is missing, socio-pedagogical work can still be meaningful. However, the ability to adequately perceive the subjective involvement in the current problem, i.e. to be as free of fear as possible and to include it in the course of the interaction, cannot be dispensed with. (cf. ibid., p. 229f)

The hallmark of all professions is a high degree of reflexivity. It is a fundamental characteristic of professional action. Reflexivity is the result of independent handling of scientific and experience-based knowledge in relation to clients, the field of work and oneself. (cf. Heiner 2004, p. 43) Heiner (2004, p. 44) defines reflexivity as "(...) the willingness and ability to systematically, methodically controlled and self-critically analyze one's own actions and the associated framework conditions (...).

Daheim (1992, cited in: Heiner 2004, p. 44) writes that reflexive action integrates three types of knowledge:

- "(...) scientific knowledge,
- professional (experience) knowledgeand
- current everyday knowledge."

The three types of knowledge are combined in relation to the task at hand and are not merely implemented and applied, but rather tested for their suitability (cf. ibid., p. 44). According to all models of professionalism and for all professions, this reflective use "(...) forms the indispensable core of competence to act" (ibid., p. 44). The competence to act is acquired during training and is subject to constant further development and safeguarding in professional practice through supervision and self-evaluation. If the relationship with the client is only goal-, task- and activity-related and there is no understanding or experience independent of agreed or set goals, a lack of self-reflexivity can be assumed. If little or no importance is attached to shaping and reflecting on the relationship between the helper and the client, and if strategic action takes precedence over understanding-oriented action, then reflection is halved, possibly even a halved intervention repertoire. (cf. ibid., p. 44ff)

Geißler and Hege (2001, p. 231) write that it is essential for professional action in social work to deal with the motives behind career choices and their examination and problematization. Training plays an enormous role in this. The motivation for training and practicing the profession is often diverse, non-specific, diffuse and in many cases changes during training or in the course of practicing the profession. (cf. ibid., p. 231) "Original opinions are recognized as rationalizations or self-disappointments when dealing critically with oneself (e.g. motives of 'wanting to help' or e.g. the motive of being able to become 'socio-politically' active)" (ibid., p. 231).

The relevance of critical reflection on past experiences is already evident during the course of study. If it is possible during training to approach one's own previous experiences openly, to accept, analyze and problematize them, then much has been gained. (cf. ibid., p. 230f) However, Geißler and Hege (2001, p. 232) are of the opinion that reflective competence can only be acquired to a limited extent during studies, as the content of professional practice can only be conveyed rationally to a large extent. The processing of such problems is reserved for in-service supervision (ibid., p. 232).

4.3.2 *Authenticity*

"'Being real, 'living authentically', actually existing' - these expressions denote something that people are striving for" (Luckner 2010, p. 6).

Thiersch (2009, p. 239) writes that the issue of authenticity is risky and points in a direction where something necessary and important can be found. Reusch (2010, p. 5) is of the opinion that the question of authenticity only becomes problematic when dealing with other people, as one always appears genuine to oneself.

"The word 'genuine' originally derives from 'legitimate': the 'real' (= legitimate son) as opposed to the illegitimate 'bastard'. In a figurative sense, it then also took on the meaning 'true', unadulterated' ('genuine' friend, 'genuine' gem)." (ibid., p. 6) In relation to people, authenticity is more of an exception, as when someone shows "their true side", this is usually worth mentioning (cf. ibid., p. 7) Luckner (2010, p. 7) is of the opinion that it is impossible to be authentic in the long term without going crazy. Authenticity is based on authentication, which means that being authentic means making oneself authentic; it is not predetermined what a person is, but rather "(...) what he made of himself in view of the circumstances of his life" (ibid., p. 8). It is not possible to look at an archetype, but to try to approach the personal design through the experiences made in the world. Authenticity or actuality corresponds to the relationship between a person's design and reality. If one is in

agreement here, one speaks of authentic, true, genuine existence. (cf. ibid., p. 8f) However, Luckner (2010, p. 7) points out that people often delude themselves about themselves, i.e. lie to themselves. Authenticity requires self-knowledge, i.e. knowing what you are or are not capable of. "Be yourself!" therefore always goes hand in hand with "Know yourself!", which is a lifelong process in which self-knowledge and personal design go hand in hand. (cf. ibid., p. 7f) "(...) Self-knowledge stands at the beginning of actual selfhood" (ibid., p. 9). Furthermore, Luckner (2010, p. 9) is of the opinion that a person's authenticity is linked to the existence of institutions. It is not beyond everyday life and institutions, but rather their modifying appropriation (authentication). Authentic possibilities open up when a person adopts forms of
practice (thus authenticating itself) or rejects it (also authenticating itself through demarcation) and attempts to establish others. The danger is that these possibilities can be lost to the authenticating institutions. Authentic selfhood is in constant danger of losing itself. (cf. ibid., p. 9) Thus, according to Luckner (2010, p. 9), authentic selfhood is only given for the moment. "Authenticity cannot be made permanent. Authentic existence, being real, only succeeds momentarily or not at all. This is precisely why free, genuine selfhood is a lifelong project." (ibid., p. 9).

Applied to social work, for Thiersch (2007, p. 36) the pedagogue must be recognizable to his or her clients. "(...) he must be credible in his pedagogical attitude, in his interest in becoming and in his balance of closeness and distance, i.e. in his problems of hope, disappointment, decision and struggles" (ibid., p. 36). It is precisely this authenticity that is a decisive factor for the success of pedagogical interaction with adolescents (cf. ibid., p. 36). In home education, helpers repeatedly have to deal with adolescents who have not yet had the experience of leaving and engaging with people. Desperate cries for recognizable people are not the exception in this field of social work. (cf. Thiersch 2010, p. 243) The authenticity and credibility of professional helpers legitimize the pedagogical process and make it possible in the first place. (cf. Luckner 2010, p. 41f) For Thiersch (2010, p. 244), passionate commitment and authenticity in pedagogical behavior represent an inner core, so to speak. Pedagogical commitment is the trigger and medium of pedagogical action. Although passion and authenticity are necessary, they are not sufficient prerequisites for pedagogical action. (cf. ibid., p. 246) Thus Thiersch (2010, p. 247) speaks of pedagogical authenticity being a moment in pedagogical action, a

necessity, but is not a prerequisite and is not tangible. "Pedagogical authenticity is related to the specifically pedagogical interest in the becoming of the other, and has its foundation in it and only in it (...)" (ibid., p. 248). Furthermore, pedagogical authenticity as action is related to a specific and delimited time or to a task. It must always be realized in the tension between commitment and release, i.e. between closeness and distance. (cf. ibid., p. 248) Thiersch (2010, p. 248) points out that life experiences, biographically acquired life patterns and problems outside of professional work have an effect on pedagogical authenticity, which in his opinion must be seen and dealt with. Thiersch (2010, p. 249) cites the compensation of one's own weakness through help as a threat to pedagogical action. By acting as helpers towards others, professionals strengthen their self-confidence.

Being close to the recipient increases the problems of authenticity. However, it is indispensable, as helpers cannot hide behind role models in their work. This proximity is therefore dependent on constant reflexivity in order not to get lost in the jungle of everyday actions and not to gamble away professionalism. (cf. ibid., p. 251f).

Summarizing thoughts and outlook

As described in the title, my work is about an examination of important aspects in a helping relationship that occur as a balance of closeness and distance in social work practice. The core thesis of this work is that the tension between closeness and distance plays an essential role in helping relationships in social work.

By way of introduction, this paper deals with professional action in social work, which is a basic condition of good social work practice. In relation to the proximity-distance problem, professional action is also located in this area of tension. As discussed in the framework model (see chapter 2.4), the professional actions and problem-solving skills of the members of the profession are decisive. This understanding of the profession implies a relationship that is oriented towards help and involves the client.

Carl R. Rogers outlined the important pillars for a functioning and successful helping relationship in his conditions for a professional relationship with the client, which he developed through his experiences with his clients. For Rogers, congruence, empathy, appreciation or positive affection and unconditional acceptance are the most important elements of a helping relationship, which create a growth-promoting climate and a meaningful working basis and are therefore important foundations of social work. These aspects of a professional helping relationship described by him are essential for relationship work and for the working alliance.

My work is about the tension between closeness and distance between helpers and clients, i.e. the polarity of closeness and distance in the helping relationship. The aspect of distance is essential for a productive relationship to succeed. While the conditions developed by Rogers tend to represent closeness to the client, detachment represents the distance necessary for the professional in a helpful relationship.

The right balance of closeness and distance is essential for the success of a professional helping relationship and serves the professional's own protection. In the literature, it represents an important working basis. If there is an imbalance between closeness and distance, the helpers quickly become overloaded and overwhelmed, which manifests itself in "burn-out" and "blunting". Mental illness, inadequate behavior and possibly even leaving the job are the consequences. Without the right balance of closeness and distance, professional social work is hardly possible. A happy medium is needed to create a boundary between the individual and the professional role.

In my work, it is extremely important to me to highlight opportunities for professionals that can promote a successful approach to the proximity-distance problem. In addition to many other competencies, I decided in my literature research to explain reflective competence and authenticity in more detail. For me personally, reflective competence and authenticity are competencies that ensure that closeness does not lead to clinging intimacy and distance does not lead to indifference and escape. In order to be able to create a balance between closeness and distance to clients and to act professionally in this area of tension, it is of immense importance that helpers consciously deal with reflexive competence and authenticity, among other things. In summary, it can be said that the tension between closeness and distance is an important part of social work. This aspect is particularly important in helping relationships. The right distance to the professional role, but also to the client, is essential for effective professional action. Since the polarity of closeness and distance in helping relationships is rarely explicitly addressed in the literature, it was important to me to have provided further food for thought on this topic with this work.

Bibliography

Books:

Asendorpf, J./Banse, R.: Psychologie der Beziehung. Bern, Göttingen, Toronto, Seattle (Verlag Hans Huber), 2000

Bimschas, B./Schröder, A.: Relationships in youth work. Study on reflective action in the profession and voluntary work. Opladen (Leske + Budrich Verlag), 2003

Dörr, M.: Relationship work. On the questionability of a fashionable term in the psychosocial field. Frankfurt am Main (Brandes & Apsel Verlag), 1996

Dörr, M./Müller, B. (eds.): Closeness and distance. A field of tension in pedagogical professionalism. Weinheim and Munich (Juventa Verlag), 2nd edition, 2007

Dörr, M./Müller, B.: Introduction. Proximity and distance as structures of professionalism in pedagogical fields of work, in: Dörr, M./Müller, B. (eds.): Nähe und Distanz. A field of tension in pedagogical professionalism. Weinheim and Munich (Juventa Verlag), 2nd edition, 2007, pp. 7-28

Geißler, K. A./Hege, M.: Konzepte sozialpädagogischen Handelns. A guide for social professions. Weinheim and Basel (Beltz Verlag), 10th, updated edition, 2001

Heiner, M.: Professionalism in social work. Theoretical concepts, models and empirical perspectives. Stuttgart (W. Kohlhammer Verlag), 2004

Heiner, M.: Social work as a profession. Cases - Fields - Skills. Munich, Basel (Ernst Reinhardt Verlag), 2007

Klatetzki, T.: Wie die Differenz von Nähe und Distanz Sinn in den Einrichtungen der Sozialen Arbeit stiftet. An organizational-theoretical interpretation, in: Dörr, M./Müller, B. (eds.): Nähe und Distanz. A field of tension in pedagogical professionalism. Weinheim and Munich (Juventa Verlag), 2nd edition, 2007, pp. 73-84

Mührel, E.: Understanding and respect. Philosophical reflections on professional attitudes in social work. Essen (Verlag DIE BLAUE EULE), 2nd, revised and expanded edition, 2008

Müller, B.: Proximity, distance, professionalism. On the logic of home education as a field of work, in: Dörr, M./Müller, B. (eds.): Nähe und Distanz. A field of tension in pedagogical professionalism. Weinheim and Munich (Ju- venta Verlag), 2nd edition, 2007, pp. 141-157

Reiners-Kröncke, W./Röhrig, S./Specht, H.: Burnout in der Sozialen Arbeit. Augsburg (Ziel Verlag), 2nd heavily revised and expanded edition, 2010

Rogers, C. R.: Development of the personality. Psychotherapy from the perspective of a therapist. Stuttgart (Klett-Cotta Verlag), 13th edition, 2000

Rogers, C. R.: Therapist and client. Fundamentals of conversational psychotherapy. Frankfurt am Main (Fischer Taschenbuch Verlag), 19th edition, 2007

Satir, V.: Communication-Self Value-Congruence. Concepts and perspectives of family therapy practice. Paderborn (Junfermann Verlag), 1990

Schmid, V.: Nähe und Distanz aus der Perspektive der Psychoanalytischen Pädagogik, in: Dörr, M./Müller, B. (eds.): Nähe und Distanz. A field of tension in educational professionalism. Weinheim and Munich (Juventa Verlag), 2nd edition, 2007, pp. 47-58

Schmidbauer, W.: The helper syndrome. Help for helpers. Reinbek near Hamburg (Rowohlt Taschenbuch Verlag), 2007

Stemmer-Lück, M.: Relationship spaces in social work. Psychoanalytic theories and their application in practice. Stuttgart (W. Kohlhammer Verlag), 2004

Stierlin, H.: The doing of one is the doing of the other. An attempt at the dynamics of human relationships. Frankfurt am Main (Suhrkamp Verlag), 2nd edition, 1972

Thiersch, H.: Nähe und Distanz in der Sozialen Arbeit, in: Dörr, M./Müller, B. (eds.): Nähe und Distanz. A field of tension in pedagogical professionalism. Weinheim and Munich (Juventa Verlag), 2nd edition, 2007, pp. 29-45

Thiersch, H.: Authentizität, in: Becker-Lenz, R./Busse, St./Ehlert, G./Müller, S. (eds.): Professionalität in der Sozialen Arbeit. Viewpoints, controversies, perspectives. Wiesbaden (VS Verlag für Sozialwissenschaften), 2009, pp. 239-253

von Spiegel, H.: Methodical action and professional competence in the field of tension between case work and management, in: Thole, W. (ed.): Grundriss Soziale Arbeit. An introductory handbook. Wiesbaden (VS Verlag für Sozialwissenschaften), 2nd, revised and updated edition, 2005, pp. 549-602

Magazines:

Luckner, A.: Become who you are! Echtheit, Authentizität, Eigentlichkeit, in: der blaue reiter. Journal for Philosophy. Issue 24, 2010

Müller, S./Becker-Lenz, R.: Der professionelle Habitus und seine Bildung in der Sozialen Arbeit, in: neue praxis. Issue 1, 2008

Reusch, S.: Echt sein, in: der blaue reiter. Journal for Philosophy. Issue 24, 2010

Other sources:

Herwig-Lempp, J. (2003): What theory does social work need? http://www. herwig-lempp.de/data/publications/0302TheorySozArbJHL.pdf (13.04.2010)

MIX
Papier aus verantwortungsvollen Quellen
Paper from responsible sources
FSC® C105338

Printed by Books on Demand GmbH, Norderstedt / Germany